Cincinnati Images

Photographs by
J. Miles Wolf

ISBN 0-9647433-5-3

Wolf Publishing Company
Cincinnati, Ohio
513.281.5580
miles@zoomtown.com
www.jmileswolf.com
www.cincygift.com

Printed in Canada

Waves of new arrivals to Cincinnati - from the Native Americans who appeared some 2,700 years ago to the early pioneers floating down the Ohio River in flatboats, from the African Americans fleeing slavery, to the European immigrants seeking prosperity - have recognized what the city's 21st-century residents know: Cincinnati is a vibrant and lively city, full of natural resources and beauty. Its big city amenities and friendly, small-town atmosphere create a quality of life that has been recognized nationally.

Today, Cincinnati is a thriving metropolitan area that has grown to almost two million people spread across parts of 3 states, Ohio, Kentucky and Indiana. The city is well-known for its cultural and educational traditions: the world class Cincinnati Symphony Orchestra, the Cincinnati Art Museum, the Museum Center at Union Terminal, and seven universities and colleges, including The University of Cincinnati, Xavier University, and Northern Kentucky University. The Cincinnati Zoo and Botanical Garden offers one of the finest conservation programs and collections of animals in the world. The city's professional and college sports teams draw fans from throughout the region, and the Cincinnati Parks system offers recreational and natural opportunities for everyone to enjoy.

Cincinnati's beauty lies in its wide river valley and hills, in its fine public art and 19th-century architecture. It also lies in the people who choose to call this river city home. I hope you enjoy this collection of photographs. It has been my pleasure and passion to photograph this area for the past 25 years.

Miles Wolf

4

Fountain Square

The heart of Cincinnati is home to the beautiful Tyler Davidson Fountain. The Fountain was made in Germany in 1871 and given as a gift to the people of Cincinnati. Today the fountain is the focal point of downtown Cincinnati and is enjoyed by residents and visitors alike. The square is a lively place where people gather for lunch, concerts, speeches, protests and festivals.

Downtown Cincinnati

This active, exciting downtown is home to many historic buildings, impressive office towers and numerous hotels. There are excellent restaurants and retail shops for people to enjoy. The new Contemporary Arts Center, left, completed in 2003 was designed by Zaha Hadid. This innovative museum has drawn international attention to downtown Cincinnati.

Universities

The University of Cincinnati, left. Is an outstanding university with world-class buildings and over 35,000 students. Xavier University, right, a Jesuit University, has a beautiful campus and over 6.500 students. Northern Kentucky University has a modern growing campus with over 15,000 students.

Cincinnati Music Hall

Designed by Samuel Hannaford and dedicated in 1878. The historic building is on the National Registrar of Historic Places.

Music Hall is home to the Cincinnati Symphony Orchestra, May Festival and the Cincinnati Opera. The magnificent grand auditorium seats 3400 people.

Cincinnati City Hall

This stately building with marble staircases and intricate stained glass windows is the center of the city government. The mayor and city council have their offices there. City Hall was designed by Samuel Hannaford and completed in 1893. Cincinnati City Hall is on the National Registrar of Historic Places.

St. Peters in Chains Cathedral

was the second permanent cathedral in the United States. It was completed in 1845. The Cathedral hosts regular masses, liturgical functions of the Archdiocese and special ceremonies like weddings and funerals.

11

Cyclists race past the Museum Center at the historic Cincinnati Union Terminal.

The Art Deco masterpiece, Cincinnati Union Terminal is now home to the Cincinnati Museum of Natural History, Cincinnati Historical Society and the Children's Museum.

Art Museums

The **Cincinnati Art Museum** has a superb collection of art spanning more than 5,000 years. The permanent collection contains masterpieces from around the world, and the temporary exhibits always excite the senses with interesting art or artifacts. The museum is located next to Mt. Adams in Eden Park.

Taft Museum, left, one of the oldest buildings in Cincinnati, built in 1820, was home to the Taft Family. In 1927 the Taft Family donated their home, their personal art collection and one million dollars to maintain the museum. The museum displays oil paintings, Chinese porcelain, antique furniture and French enamels. Lytle Park adds a beautiful green space and flower gardens in front of the museum.

The Aronoff Center

Home to the Cincinnati Ballet, concerts and numerous Broadway plays. This performing arts center was designed by Cesar Pelli, it opened in 1995.
The Aronoff Center for the Arts consists of three performance spaces and an art gallery.

(Right) The Cincinnati Ballet performs during the grand opening of the Aronoff Center.

Festivals

Oktoberfest and the Taste of Cincinnati are great traditions in Cincinnati. The weekend festivals draw hundreds of thousands of people to downtown Cincinnati. Oktoberfest celebrates Cincinnati's German heritage with beer, food, music and dancing. It is the largest Oktoberfest celebration outside of Munich, Germany. Right, crowds enjoy local food at the Taste of Cincinnati.

The Nation Underground Railroad Freedom Center welcomes visitors from around the world to Cincinnati's riverfront. It has fantastic exhibits that tell the story of slavery and freedom.

The Black Family Reunion at Sawyer Point park draws over 250,000 people..

The Great American Ball Park is the new home of the Cinicnnati Reds. The Ball Park opened in 2003 and has provided the setting for many exciting major league baseball games.

The Crosley Terrace entrance to Great American Ball Park reminds fans of the great history of the Cincinnati Reds, baseball's first professional team.

The 65,000 seat Paul Brown Stadium opened for the Cincinnati Bengals 2000 season.

Ohio River view to the East from Mt. Echo Park.

The Ohio River with a golden autumn view from Walnut Hills. The cities of Dayton, Newport and Covington line the Kentucky shoreline.

The John A. Roebling Suspension Bridge was begun in 1856 and completed in 1867. It was the first bridge to span the Ohio River and it is still in operation today.

Ohio River view from Eden Park.

Boats gather on the Ohio River for the annual Riverfest fireworks festival.

Mt. Adams overlooks the Ohio River Valley at sunset.

A coal laden barge navigates the fog and the Ohio River bridges near Cincinnati's Public Landing.

Serpentine Wall in Yeatman's Cove Park is a popular riverfront destination.

The Ohio River reflects the Cincinnati skyline.

Cincinnati Zoo and Botanical Garden

One of the top zoos in the United States. It is famous for it's white tigers and successful breeding programs. The zoo began operating at its present location in 1875. The Elephant House, left, is on the National Register of Historic Places.

Cincinnati Parks

One of the jewels of Cincinnati is the wonderful park system.

At over 5,000 acres it is one of the largest and finest collections of urban parks in the United States. Abraham Lincoln statue in downtown's Lytle Park.

Left, ice skating on Mirror Lake in Eden park.

Ault Park Pavilion hosts free concerts, private weddings and special events. Ault Park is one of Cincinnati's finest public parks, featuring gardens, overlooks, playgrounds, woods and trails.

Mt Airy Forest is Cincinnati's finest nature preserve, and at 1469 acres includes plenty of woods, streams, valleys, gardens and wildlife.

Krohn Conservatory, built in 1933, is a wonderful building that houses a waterfall and an amazing collection of plants. It is located in Eden Park.

Fresh snow surrounds the Water Tower atop Eden Park. The view includes the Ohio River, Cincinnati Art Museum, Mt. Adams and Downtown Cincinnati.

Coney Island, a destination of Cincinnatians for over 100 years. The area now features Sunlight Pool, children's rides, Riverbend Music Center and Summerfair.

The Mini-Heart Marathon runs down Columbia Parkway in front of Mt. Adams.

Mt. Adams

An upscale neighborhood of historic homes, restaurants and shops. Home to Eden Park, Cincinnati Art Museum and Playhouse in the Park. The landmark Immaculata Church, is the site of a 140 year tradition, the Good Friday pilgrimage, where thousands of people climb the stairs, saying a prayer on each step.

Neighborhoods

Cincinnati's neighborhoods give the city its character. From the Victorian charm of Tusculum, far left, to the historic mansions of Clifton, North Avondale and Northside. Hyde Park Square, left, welcomes visitors to its small shops and dining. The country estates of Indian Hill, Maderia and Terrace Park are surrounded by woods and horse trails.

Covington, Kentucky's riverfront features spectacular views of the Cincinnati skyline from the Ascent at Roebling's Bridge, Rivercenter and several hotels.

Cathedral Basilica of the Assumption. This magnificent church is modeled after Notre Dame in Paris. It's 2001-2002 renovation restored and updated the Cathedral.

Newport on the Levee is Newport Kentucky's new entertainment complex, featuring an aquarium, restaurants, nightclubs and movie theaters.

Riverfront dining on the banks of the Ohio River.
Newport, Covington and Cincinnati all have excellent riverside restaurants.

Over the Rhine, settled by German immigrants, this historic neighborhood is a dramatic mix of nightclubs, small businesses and poverty. Music Hall is featured in the background.

Fresh fruits, vegetables and meats have been available at Findlay Market since 1852. It is a tradition in many Cincinnati families to shop at the market every weekend.

President James Garfield oversees a lunch time crowd in downtown's Piatt Park.

Sunrise over the Ohio River as viewed from Eden Park.

Moonrise over Cincinnati.

Cincinnati's riverboat heritage is celebrated at Tall Stacks. The largest gathering of riverboats in the world delights visitors at Serpentine Wall.

Tall Stacks Festival comes only once every four years. It draws over 600,000 people to the riverfronts of Cincinnati, Newport, and Covington.

Riverfest fireworks delight 500,000 viewers every Labor Day. The local Rozzi family produces one of the largest annual fireworks displays in the world.

Kings Island

Kings Island offers more than 80 rides and attractions. The amusement park features the longest wooden roller coaster in the world and the newest in children's attractions and rides. Kings Island offers fun for the entire family. Fireworks are featured nightly near their huge replica of the Eiffel Tower.